Egon Schiele

PARK
LANE

HIS WORKS

Egon Schiele
HIS LIFE AND WORKS

Egon Schiele lived for only twenty-eight years, but it was during a crucial period in contemporary history, a period in which great and violent upheavals marked the beginning of the twentieth century. Austria, his homeland, was the center of activity. Vienna, with its population of more than two million, was the fourth largest city in Europe and was a strategic crossroads— and often a source—of the continent's turmoil. Among those living and working there were Gustav Klimt, Oskar Kokoschka, Sigmund Freud, Karl Kraus, Stefan Zweig, Alfred Loos, Richard Krafft-Ebing, Josef Hoffmann, Gustav Mahler, Arthur Schnitzler, Ludwig Wittgenstein, Arnold Schönberg, Josef Stalin, and Adolf Hitler.

Schiele's art seems to convey the depth and spirit of the atmosphere. It is full of the kind of charged energy that is felt before a storm and that must have characterized the last, glorious days of the Austrian capital. His complex personality was molded by the tensions felt by people at the fin de siècle—their fears, their triumphs, and their defeats.

Field of Flowers
(Detail)

Egon Leo Adolf Schiele was born on June 12, 1890, in Tulln, a small town near Vienna, to Adolf Eugen Schiele, of German origin, and his wife, Marie Soukoup. The third of four children, Egon had three sisters, Elvira (who died in 1893), Melanie, and Gertrud, who frequently posed as a model for him.

Schiele's father was the local stationmaster and the family lived on the second floor of the railroad station. It is not surprising, therefore, that Schiele's earliest drawings are of railroad trains and carriages.

His formal education began at Tulln's primary school, but when he was eleven years old he went to stay with relatives in Krems to attend secondary school, since there was none in Tulln. He later went to Klosterneuburg, in the outskirts of Vienna, where, toward the end of 1904, his family moved.

Egon, like his father and paternal grandfather, had a talent for drawing, and his artistic studies began in 1905, when the painter Ludwig Karl Strauch, a former pupil of the Fine Arts Academy in Vienna, started teaching at the Klosterneuburg school. He immediately noticed his pupil's precocious talent (although his performance was poor in all the other subjects, except calligraphy and gymnastics). Strauch took a special interest in the boy, giving him private lessons and the opportunity to paint in his studio. There and outdoors in the fields, Schiele practiced painting classical themes: still lifes, landscapes, portraits of his teacher and his family, religious themes, and self-portraits.

On January 1 of that year, Schiele's father had died. Apart from creating economic difficulties for the family, and aggravating Egon's already difficult relationship with his mother, his father's death made him the "man of the family." Perhaps this situation led him to the narcissism demonstrated by the large number of self-portraits.

With the support of Strauch and of the painter Max Kahrer, and against the wishes of his mother and of his uncle, godfather, and guardian Leopold Czihaczek, in 1906 Schiele enrolled in the course given by Christian Griepenkerl at the Vienna

Academy of Art. Here, after a period of diligence and enthusiasm—partly to please his uncle and guardian who rarely denied him loans or refused to pose for him—he soon clashed with the teaching system that concentrated mainly on copying old paintings. Griepenkerl, who was famous at the time for his very old-fashioned historical paintings, required his students to do boring exercises that left little scope for individual creativity or for the imagination. The work Schiele did at the academy reveals practically nothing of his talent. But his talent was strengthened by the experience, and his style did not suffer at all. And far more important to him was his discovery in 1907 of the work of Gustav Klimt and the other artists who had formed the Association of Austrian Painters Secession (in the sense of secession from the academy).

Schiele met Klimt that same year, probably in one of the cafés he had begun to frequent, where it was not difficult to meet prominent people from the art world. Just as in Paris during the golden age of Impressionism, the cafés were an essential part of cultural life in Vienna at the fin de siècle, and two of them became particularly famous—the Café Tivoli and the Café Museum, designed by Adolf Loos and close to the Secession Palace. Klimt, who was forty-five and already a well-known painter, was favorably impressed by Schiele, who was only seventeen years old. He agreed to exchange some drawings with him, offered him some words of encouragement, and, with his usual generosity, introduced him to important patrons of art and to the Wiener Werkstätte. The Wiener Werkstätte were founded in 1903 by Koloman Moser, Josef Hoffmann, and Fritz Warndorfer, with Klimt's support, and in their own shops they produced and sold all kinds of applied-art objects, promoting a new and sophisticated design in Austria as well as abroad.

Klimt's influence over the young painter's style during that period is quite evident, as can be seen in drawings like the one on the greeting card he did for his aunt in 1907 or in *Water Spirits I*, of the same year, which recalls Klimt's newly finished *Water Snakes*.

Schiele was not influenced by Klimt alone. He experimented with various styles and tried to find a style of his own. He began working for the Wiener Werkstätte toward the end of 1908. There he created cards and designed some clothes, and even managed (this time with Josef Hoffmann's help) to get his sister Gerti a job as a model. His first opportunity to exhibit his work came in May of the same year, with an exhibition at Klosterneuburg, in the Augustinian monastery. Schiele's ten paintings, exhibited along with works by local but well-known artists, caught the eye of Heinrich Benesch, who was to play an important role in Schiele's life, as a confidant as well as a sponsor.

Another, more important exhibition was held in Vienna that summer: the first Kunstschau, organized by the Klimt group, which had recently resigned from the Secession; it was held temporarily in an area planned by Josef Hoffmann. Many artists from the Wiener Werkstätte and the Kunstgewerbschule exhibited there in what the group liked to define as "a complete artwork"; among them were Kokoschka and Klimt himself, who presented sixteen paintings. Needless to say, Schiele visited the exhibition and was again fascinated by the famous painter's latest works; to some extent, the older painter's influence is more apparent in Schiele's 1909 works than in those of two years earlier.

The continuing differences of opinion between Griepenkerl and his pupils caused Schiele and his fellow students to write their professor a letter containing thirteen questions in which they contested his methods and the methods and aims of the whole academy. This occurred in the summer of 1909, and shortly afterward Schiele obtained a mediocre third-year diploma and left the academy, at the same time declining his guardian's hospitality, and moved into an apartment in the Alserbachstrasse.

With some friends who had left the academy with him, Schiele founded the Newkunstgruppe (New Art Group), of which he was elected president. The sixteen members (among

Female Nude
(Detail)

14

them was Anton Peschka, who married Egon's sister Gertrud in 1912) decided to organize a collective exhibition at the Galerie Pisko, planning to present six works each. During this time Schiele received an invitation, again from Klimt, to take part in the second Kuntschau, which was held during those months. Schiele exhibited four paintings, three of them portraits, that went almost unnoticed. Also shown were paintings by Kokoschka, Slegovt, Munch, Khnopff, Toorop, Bonnard, Matisse, van Gogh, and Gauguin.

The first exhibition arranged by the Neukunstgruppe, which had in the meantime gained two new artists (one of them, Albert Paris von Gütersloh, was among the first to write about Schiele), was well attended and enabled the young painter to meet Arthur Roessler, a future supporter. A writer and art critic for the *Arbeiter Zeitung*, with extremely innovative and liberal ideas, Roessler in his article on the Newkunstgruppe exhibition declared Schiele to be "extraordinarily gifted" and introduced him to the industrialist Carl Reininghaus and the surgeon Oskar Reichel. Both were well-known and wealthy collectors; Reichel, for example, owned works by Manet, Gauguin, Kokoschka, Munch, van Gogh, and Toulouse-Lautrec. Schiele was most fascinated by Toulouse-Lautrec's work, which he had discovered the previous year in an exhibition at the Galerie Miethke. *The Evil One*, which Schiele painted in 1910, clearly shows how much his art in that period was influenced by the French artist.

But Arthur Roessler's interest in Schiele did not end there. Before the end of the year he introduced him to the publisher Eduard Kosmack and obtained some commissions for him. Schiele painted as many as eleven portraits on commission: for Kosmack, for the gynecologist von Graff, for Reichel; he portrayed Herbert Rainer, son of a university professor, and Roessler himself. The famous architect Otto Wagner also sat for him, but after a few sittings, evidently finding the painter's style disconcerting, Wagner stopped going to the studio, upsetting Schiele's plans to paint a series of portraits of some of the most prominent contemporary cultural figures in Vienna.

Undoubtedly, the 1910 portraits show a violent acquisition of highly personal styles and characteristics. Schiele's brush strokes imply a ruthless investigation of his subjects' innermost thoughts and a desire to disclose their secrets.

At the end of 1910 he met Heinrich Benesch, a collector with fairly limited financial resources who spent most of his money on paintings. In a letter he begged Schiele not to throw away any of his sketches, however imperfect or incomplete they were, but to keep them for him. He, too, was to become one of Schiele's unquestioning admirers and was painted by him in 1913, with his son Otto, a future art historian and director of the Albertina.

Schiele's relationship with his guardian and uncle Leopold Czihaczek had become strained despite Leopold's continued financial support. Ties were severed entirely when Schiele left for Krumau (now Cesky Krumlov in the Czech Republic), his mother's native town, with Erwin Osen, an eccentric actor and painter who was a member of the Neukunstgruppe, and Osen's companion, Moa. Osen's expressive and somewhat contorted theatrical gestures were a source of inspiration for the gestural movements in Schiele's own paintings, and through Osen he became acquainted with the work of Arthur Rimbaud, which was his introduction to poetry.

He exhibited a painting at the Internationale Jagdausstellung in Vienna, with the help of Josef Hoffmann, and in the autumn he took part in a new exhibition in Klosterneuburg. In November he moved to a new studio on the Grünbergstrasse.

He returned to Krumau again in 1911, this time with seventeen-year-old Valerie Neuzil, called Wally, who had already posed for Klimt. Wally became Schiele's lover and was the model for some of his best erotic drawings. Unfortunately all that is known about her is what can be learned from these drawings. Certainly, however, her sensuality unleashed a passion that Schiele had never before experienced.

This unusual couple soon attracted malicious gossip in the little provincial town, and they were forced to return to Vienna,

*The Artist's
Room in
Neulengbach*
(Detail)

17

settling in Sobieskigasse. Schiele was disappointed, but also proud. His "forced exile" strengthened his conviction that he was special, and showed him that he was not mistaken in thinking himself different from (and therefore superior to) the masses.

He immediately looked for a new residence outside Vienna, and found it at Neulengbach, a rural area that was thirty minutes by train from the capital. Here, fascinated by the nature of the place, he painted many landscapes and some views of the town, without its inhabitants, calling it Dead Town. He also experimented, successfully and undoubtedly to his personal satisfaction, with painting on wood: among his most successful works are *The Artist's Room in Neulengbach*, and *Self-Portrait with Black Clay Vase*, both done in 1911. The first, clearly inspired by the *Artist's Bedroom in Arles* by van Gogh, which Schiele had had the opportunity of admiring in one of his patrons' collections, has the painter's signature and the date on it in three places, but this is not unusual; Schiele generally wrote his name on everything he possessed, and wrote at least one signature and date on his paintings. This not only helps to reconstruct his life, but also reveals an interesting facet of his personality.

Equally interesting is the *Self-Portrait with Black Clay Vase*: the vase depicts a male head and appears at the same height as Schiele's face, almost as though it were revealing a second, secret and obscure identity. The first publications about Schiele came out during the year, written by Arthur Roessler and Albert Paris von Gütersloh.

In September 1911, with the help of Arthur Roessler, he contacted Hans Goltz, a famous Munich art dealer who was always interested in recent trends and who was already acquainted with the newly founded Blaue Reiter (Blue Rider, a name taken from a painting by Kandinsky to baptize a group that included Klee, Kandinsky, Marc, and Macke, among others). The Delphin Verlag commissioned Schiele to do a lithograph that was to be included in a portfolio from the Sema Club, of which Alfred Kubin, Paul Klee, and Max Oppenheimer were also members.

Oppenheimer's portrait was painted by Schiele the previous year. The *Sema Portfolio* came out in January 1912.

Various drawings belong to the period spent in Neulengbach, especially erotic ones of children and adolescents, who were visibly amused at the idea of being painted, and happy to escape from the vigilance of their parents to a house where they could explore and enjoy themselves. The painter was pleased to welcome them and they were equally happy to undress for his drawings.

Here too, as in Krumau, stories and rumors about Schiele began to spread until he was finally denounced. It seemed that the painter had seduced one of his young models, the thirteen-year-old Tatjana Georgette von Mossig. About a hundred paintings were confiscated, and on April 13, 1910, while investigations got under way, Schiele was sent to prison. The trial ended with the public destruction of one of the incriminating drawings and the withdrawal of the main accusation, but the charge of having created and shown "pornographic" material to the children was maintained, for which the artist had to serve a three-day prison sentence. Actually he had already spent two weeks in prison, awaiting trial, part of the time in Neulengbach and the rest at Sankt Pölten. Had he been found guilty of corruption of minors, he could have been sentenced to as long as twenty years at hard labor.

While in custody Schiele did not remain idle. Although he had no mirrors with him, he painted a series of self-portraits and several views of his prison cells. In these self-portraits he reached the peak of his self-commiseration. Beneath the signature and date there are often short sentences that could well be used as titles: "I do not feel punished, but cleansed!". . . "I will survive for art and for the people I love!". . . "It is a crime to set limits for an artist, it means putting an end to a new life!". . . "Art cannot be modern: art is eternal," and others.

Soon Schiele presented his works at the Neukunstgruppe's second and last collective exhibition, held at the Künstlerhaus in Budapest in January, and at Hans Goltz's gallery in February

*Heinrich and
Otto Benesch*
(Detail)

and March, alongside the Blaue Reiter painters. In spring he participated in the Sonderbund in Cologne. It was a great event, the most important modern art exhibition ever organized: there were the artists from the Die Brucke group (their last time together), almost all the members of the Blaue Reiter, Kokoschka, and many others, particularly the Impressionists. In July Schiele presented seven works at the Vienna exhibition of the Hagenband, a group that had left the Secession, and on that occasion he met two new collectors, the industrialist August Lederer, owner of a distillery in Györ (in what is now Hungary) and Klimt's patron, and Franz Hauer, owner of a famous beer house in Vienna.

The following month Schiele was in Munich. There he bought a copy of the Blaue Reiter almanac and manifesto and wrote down in a notebook the names of the galleries and artists in whom he was most interested. Among these were Nolde, Marc, Klee, Kirchner, Jawlensky, and Rops.

On returning to Vienna he moved with Wally into his new studio, at Number 101 of the Hiepzinger Haupstrasse, in a pleasant neighborhood. He spent Christmas 1912 at the home of the Lederer family in Györ, where he painted a portrait of their third son, fifteen-year-old Erich. Schiele was amused and flattered by the attentions he received from the wealthy and educated members of high society whom he met.

A unique painting called *The Bridge* belongs to the period Schiele spent in Hungary. It clearly shows that he continually experimented with new techniques and styles; the bridge, depicted with extreme punctilious accuracy, rich details, and a careful study of perspective, contrasts violently with the river and the barge navigating along it. The river and the barge are reduced to flat, two-dimensional figures, difficult to situate in space; they are almost abstract.

Another extremely interesting painting, again dated 1913, is the double portrait of *Heinrich and Otto Benesch*, which was purchased by Carl Reininghaus. It unites the accuracy of the portrait with the drama of the scene, once again penetrating further

*Seated Woman
with Hand in Hair*
(Detail)

into the depths of a situation than is normally possible; the elderly collector places his arm protectively between his almost grown-up son and the observer-painter.

In January Schiele joined the Bund Österreichischer Kunstler—the league of Austrian artists of which Gustav Klimt had been president since the previous year—and in March he exhibited in Budapest with the other members of the association. He also took part in the Munich Secession exhibition, in spring, at the Viennese Internationale Scheanzweissausstellung and at the Grosse Deutsche Kunstausstellung in Berlin. There he met Franz Pfemfert, director of *Die Aktion*, the weekly review of politics, literature, and art, who asked him to contribute drawings and texts. He also participated in the forty-third exhibition of the Viennese Secession, and at the beginning of the summer Hanz Goltz organized a personal exhibition for him in his Munich gallery.

Thanks yet again to Goltz's intercession, works by Schiele were exhibited at the beginning of 1914 in Dresden, Hamburg, Cologne, and Stuttgart. For the first time, too, his paintings went outside German-speaking countries: he exhibited in Rome and Paris among other places. He also participated in a collective exhibition at the Galerie Pisko. The judges, who awarded the prize to Albert Paris von Gütersloh, included Klimt, Josef Hoffmann, and von Reininghaus, who promoted and sponsored the exhibition.

In the spring Schiele received lessons in engraving from Robert Philippi, and in the summer he tried etching for the first time, successfully completing six works, including a portrait of Roessler, who had given him the equipment. However, the patience and dedication that were required soon made him lose interest, and he did not try this technique again.

A few months earlier he had been fascinated by another mechanical technique: photography. He had had portraits taken of himself by the photographer Anton Josef Treka, frequently in poses reminiscent of the gestural quality of his own self-portraits. Schiele sometimes worked on these photographs with his paintbrush and then signed them. The profile that emerges is quite fascinating: Egon Schiele was undoubtedly a good-looking man, and the refined narcissist in him delighted in studying new, unexpected poses, appearing alternately grotesque or thoughtful, motionless or in almost acrobatic poses, displaying a confident mastery over the expressiveness of his whole body, not just his face.

During these months Schiele noticed the Harms sisters, Edith and Adele, who lived in the building opposite him. First he would wave at them, shouting across the road or showing his self-portraits at the window. Then he sent them notes that went unanswered for a long time, and finally he visited them, with Wally as an involuntary accomplice, since the girls' parents would probably not have allowed them to go out with him alone. A letter he wrote in February 1915 to Arthur Roessler revealed his intentions: he had decided to marry, without mentioning a name, but to his "advantage," and in any case it would not be Wally. He broke off with her in the spring, but it was not easy: she had lived with him for four years and had been close to him during his imprisonment; she had seen him mature artistically and had inspired some of his finest paintings. Undoubtedly their physical relationship had been excellent, quite different from his relationship with his future wife. This can be immediately discerned from a comparison between paintings like *Wally in a Red Blouse Lying on Her Back*, dated 1913, and *Portrait of Edith Harms*, painted in 1915. It was Edith whom Schiele had decided to marry, after Adele declared herself to be "a veritable nun." This declaration did not prevent Adele from posing, partially undressed, for her brother-in-law, perhaps demonstrating a sensuality and confidence that her sister did not possess.

In the meantime, war had broken out. Initially Schiele had been declared unfit because of his weak constitution, and this had enabled him to continue to paint regularly throughout 1914, and to participate in two exhibitions, both of them at the beginning of 1915. The first was at the Kunsthaus in Zurich,

Portrait of
Johann Harms
(Detail)

and the second at the Galerie Arnot in Vienna, where he exhibited sixteen oils and several watercolors and drawings. Schiele designed the poster for the exhibition, portraying himself as St. Sebastian pierced by long spears.

But Schiele was finally drafted into military service and left for Prague on June 21, 1915, four days after his wedding in the Evangelic and Lutheran church in Vienna; his mother was not present. Before leaving he met Wally at the Eichberger Café, which he used to frequent, and suggested that they continue to see each other, without Edith's knowledge, every summer. Wally refused and soon left the city. They did not meet again; she died of scarlet fever in December 1917, after joining the Red Cross as a nurse. Schiele's deep affection for her had not ceased, however: the pain of separation was a silent cry emanating from *Pregnant Woman and Death*, dated 1915. The painting was visibly inspired by Klimt's *The Embrace*: the man depicted seems to be embracing and at the same time pushing away a woman who is trying to restrain him with her thin, weak arms. The man's face, which has Schiele's features, shows resignation and dismay. Edith followed her husband to Prague and stayed at the Hotel Paris.

In Prague Schiele suffered under the strict military discipline that hardly suited his style of living. His continuous protests led to his transfer to Vienna, where he was engaged initially in fortification work, and then he volunteered to escort convoys of prisoners from the capital to a nearby concentration camp.

The violence of war does not enter Schiele's paintings. His painting was already, prophetically, full of a sense of imminent drama. Even when he portrayed soldiers, their grief was individual and private. His creative rhythm slowed down, however, since he obviously had less time to dedicate to his art. He painted only eleven pictures in 1915, and eight in 1916. Nonetheless, he exhibited two works at the Bund Osterreichischer Kunstler exhibition at the Berlin Secession, at the Vienna Kunstschau, and at the Munich Secession. Goltz organized another personal exhibition for him in his Munich gallery, and he sent some drawings to Dresden for an exhibition of the local artistic association. Another exhibition was to be held at Guido Arnot's gallery, but relations between Arnot and Schiele were not good and the project was abandoned.

In the spring Egon Schiele was sent to a military detachment in Muhling bei Weiselburg in southern Austria, where there was a prisoner-of-war camp, to do an office job. Edith followed him. There his superiors soon noticed his artistic talent and supplied him with a space in a warehouse that he could transform into a makeshift studio. There he painted a *View of Krumau*, *The Ruined Mill at Muhling*, and *Russian Soldier*. The war seemed incredibly remote: the colors are brighter and the whirling, foaming water, no longer imprisoned by the abandoned mill, is a triumph of vitality. Krumau itself, previously painted as a gloomy and lifeless landscape, becomes a bright and even cheerful village. The *Portrait of Johann Harms*, depicting his elderly father-in-law, was painted the same year. Instead of sitting, the old man looks as though he has been thrown onto the hard wooden chair, his hoary head resting on one hand. The legs are excluded from the picture, as frequently happens in Schiele's paintings, but this time the implications were probably different: the man seems about to slide off the chair and out of the picture, out of life, leaving behind him only his wide coat, in which he appears shrunken and withered.

In September of the same year the magazine *Die Aktion*, to which Schiele had continued to contribute, dedicated a special issue to him, an honor that the editor and director Pfemfert granted to very few painters. The issue included a poem and seven drawings by the artist, including a self-portrait on the front page and a *Portrait of the Painter Felix Harta*. It also contained an essay on Schiele by Ulrik Brendel and Heinrich Nowak. Although it had a small circulation, *Die Aktion*, together with *Der Sturm*, was the most important Expressionist periodical, defending left-wing political views and pacifism. The special issue contributed considerably to Schiele's growing fame in Germany.

Soon afterward, in January 1917, Schiele was transferred to Vienna, to the Kaiserlich-Königlich Konsumanstalt für die Armee im Felde (Royal Imperial Commissariat for the Troops in the Field, an organization that supplied food, alcohol, and tobacco to the troops), probably through the intercession of the official and collector Karl Grunwald. Schiele's superior, Hans von Rosé, asked him to do a series of drawings depicting the offices and warehouses where he worked; the drawings were intended for a publication that never actually materialized. Permission to sleep at home enabled Schiele to return, at least part of the time, to his normal working rhythm: that year he produced thirteen paintings and a large number of drawings. He also participated successfully in numerous exhibitions: in Stockholm and Copenhagen, at a venue sponsored by the government, in Amsterdam, at the Munich Secession, at the Francisco Carolino Museum in Linz. In May he exhibited at the Kreigsausstellung held at the Vienna Prater, along with Albert Paris von Gutersloh. The Moderne Galerie, the public museum of Vienna, bought a series of his drawings. In July an album containing twelve reproductions of his works was published by Richard Lanyi, and in the same month the *Neues Wiener Journal* published an enthusiastic article about him. In June he went with Grunwald to the south Tyrol to do some of the drawings commissioned by von Rosé. In addition, during the year he had planned to found an artists' association, the Kunsthalle, convinced that it should have a hand in the postwar reconstruction of the country.

With the death of Klimt, on February 6, 1918, Schiele became the most acclaimed Austrian artist. Kokoschka, who had always been in competition with him, was seriously wounded in Dresden. Schiele did three portraits of Klimt and wrote his obituary for the new periodical *Der Anbruch*.

As though in recognition of his triumph, the decision was reached by the Viennese Secession to make Schiele's works the centerpiece of its forty-ninth exhibition. The entire central hall was dedicated to him, and he exhibited almost fifty drawings and paintings. He also designed the poster, which clearly alluded to the Last Supper. A similar scene had been the subject of an unfinished painting where, in the place opposite the one occupied in all probability by Schiele himself, sat an almost bald figure: with the death of Klimt, Schiele had lost a teacher, friend, and supporter. The exhibition was a triumph, and he sold most of his works for prices they had never commanded before. The newspapers acknowledged his worth: the reviews were more favorable than ever. In April he and the other painters were transferred to the military museum in Vienna (the present Heeresgeschichtliches Museum), to save them from the dangers of the front.

Toward the end of spring he presented four works at the Zurich Kunsthaus for the exhibition "A Century of Viennese Painting," and the prices asked for his paintings rose still higher when he exhibited again at the Galerie Arnot in May. In the same month he also exhibited two hundred drawings and designs at the Kunstlerhaus Rudolphinum in Prague and in the Arnold gallery in Dresden. He received so many commissions that he had to employ a secretary to deal with all his correspondence. Egon and Edith moved again, this time to a small house with a large studio in Wattmanngasse, in the borough of Heitzing.

The same influenza epidemic that had killed Klimt caused the death of Edith, who was six months pregnant, on October 28. Egon Schiele died of influenza three days later on October 31, 1918, in his father-in-law's house. He was twenty-eight years old, at the peak of his development and creativity.

The Family, completed earlier that year, is considered his spiritual testament and depicts the yearning for something the tormented painter never knew. It shows a naked man and woman with a child. The child is protected between the legs of his mother, who is protected in the same way by the man, who is Schiele. Their bodies, naked but tangible, with more solid muscles than Schiele usually portrayed, are surrounded by darkness that appears, if not threatening, at least unfathomable. The three

The Family
(Detail)

of them in their strange, silent, fearful communion, are all look-
ing in different directions. A fragile balance has been reached in
this painting.

Egon Schiele died on the same day that the victors of World
War I decreed the end of the Austro-Hungarian Empire. The
myth he created about himself, which was extended by Arthur
Roessler after his death, transformed Schiele into one of the
most acclaimed painters of the twentieth century—although his
place in the history of art was questioned for a long time. While
it is true that much of the interest in Schiele derives from the
erotism of his pictures, it is equally true that his pictorial
achievement was important: Egon Schiele experienced and
unconsciously told the story of the end of one world and the
birth of another.

Portrait of Gertrude Schiele

Portrait of the Painter Hans Massman

Sunflower

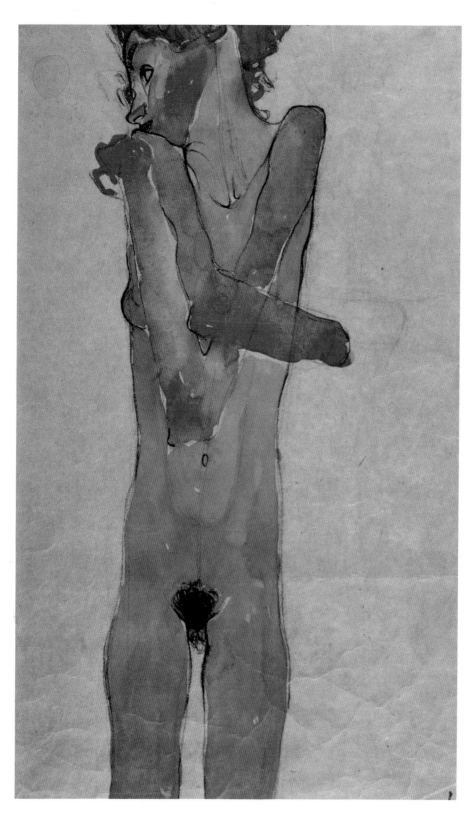

Standing Girl, Nude, with Crossed Arms

Nude Girl (Detail)

Seated Girl

Nude Boy Standing

Girl Kneeling

Portrait of Arthur Roessler

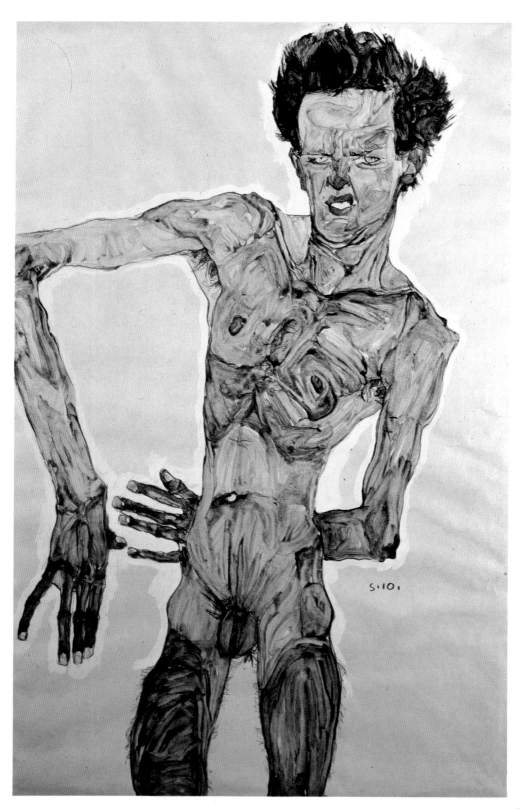

Nude Self-Portrait, Grimacing

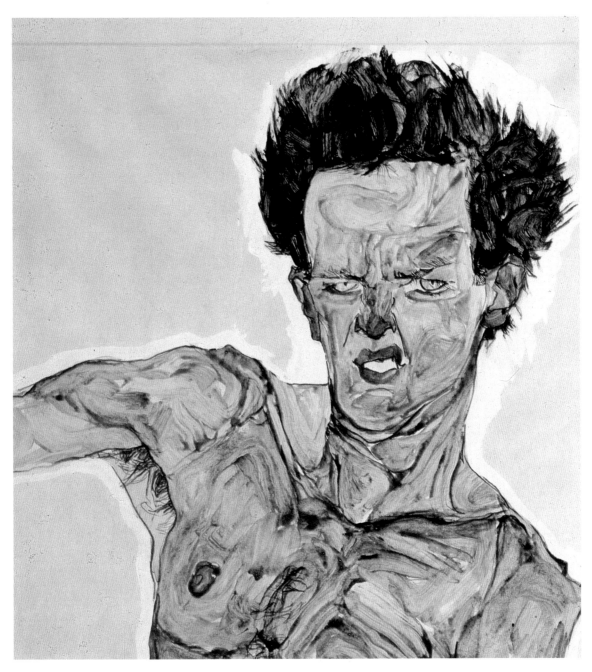

Self-Portrait (Detail)

Self-Portrait with Tooth

Self-Portrait (Detail)

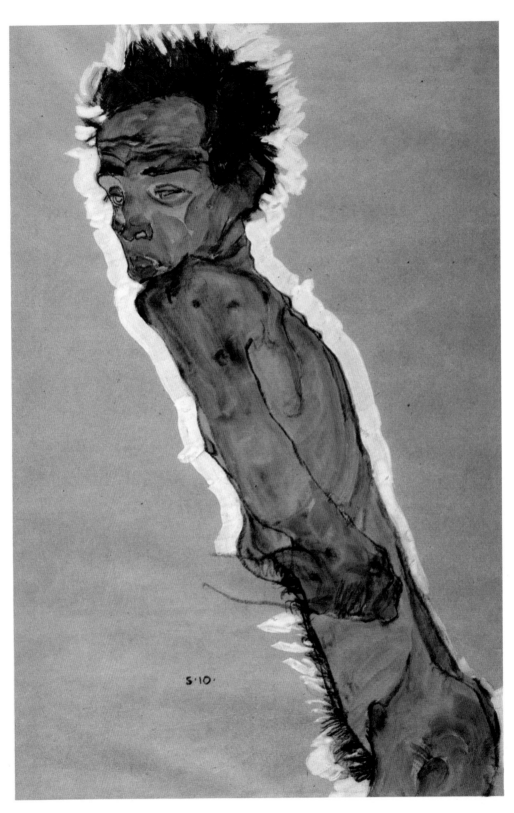

Leaning Male Nude (Self-Portrait)

Reclining Girl

Nude Black-haired Girl

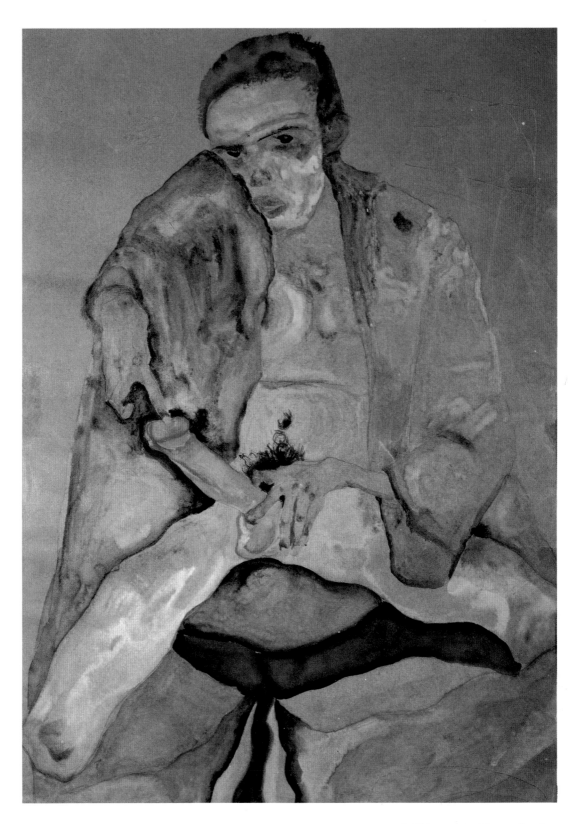

Self-Portrait Masturbating

Autumn Trees

Pregnant Woman and Death

Self-Portrait with Black Clay Vase

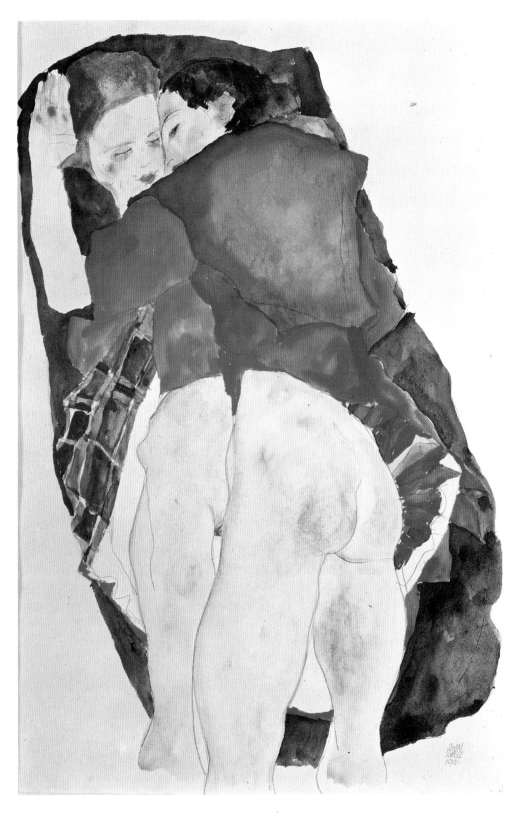

Lovers

Lovers (Detail)

Seated Woman

Krumau

Old City

Self-Portrait as Prisoner

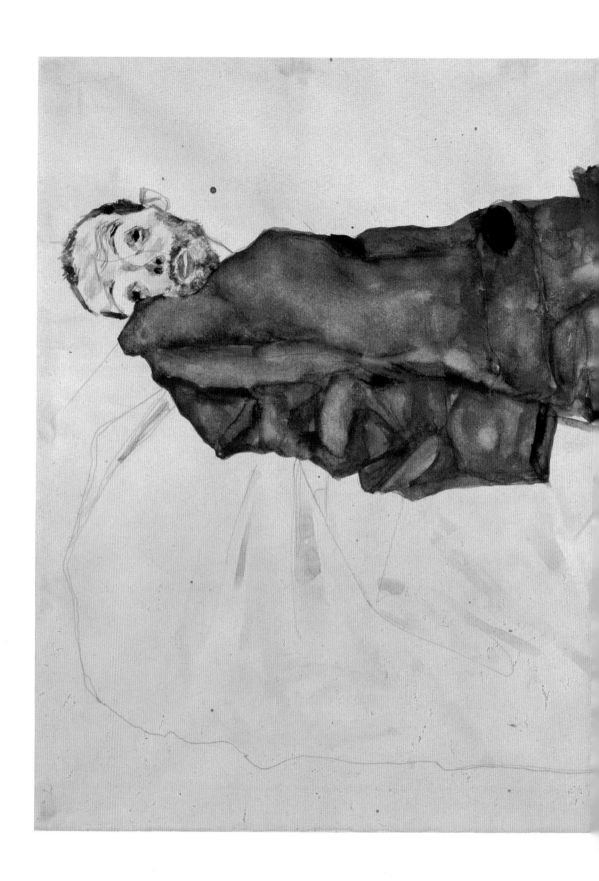

Self-Portrait as Prisoner

Organic Movement of Chair and Jug

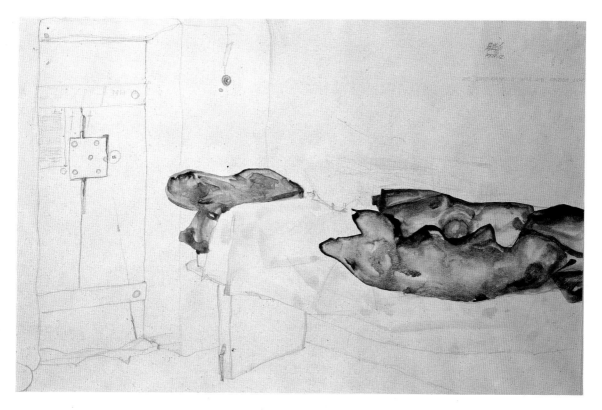

'The One Orange was the Only Light'

Prison Passage

The Door into the Open

'Art Cannot be Modern: Art is Eternal'

Trieste Fishing Boats

Heinrich and Otto Benesch

Little Town: Krumau on the Moldau

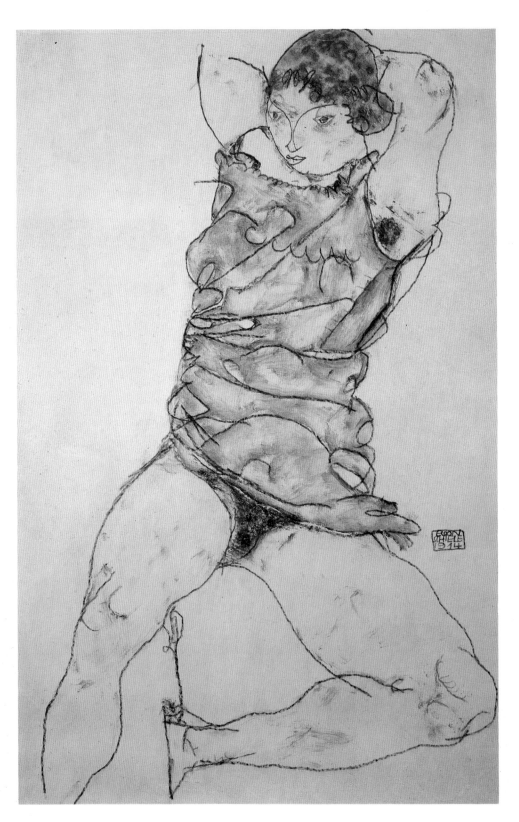

Reclining Girl

Standing Girl

Nude

Young Mother

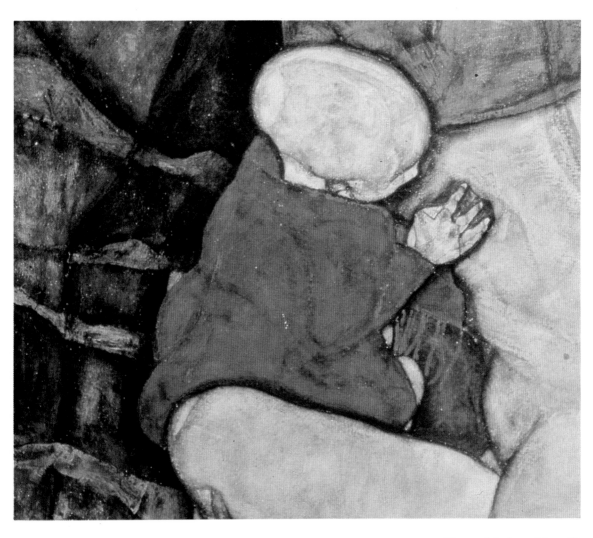

Young Mother (Detail)

Reclining Woman with Green Stockings

Two Girls Embracing

Two Girls Embracing (Detail)

View of Krumau

Town Quarter of Krumau

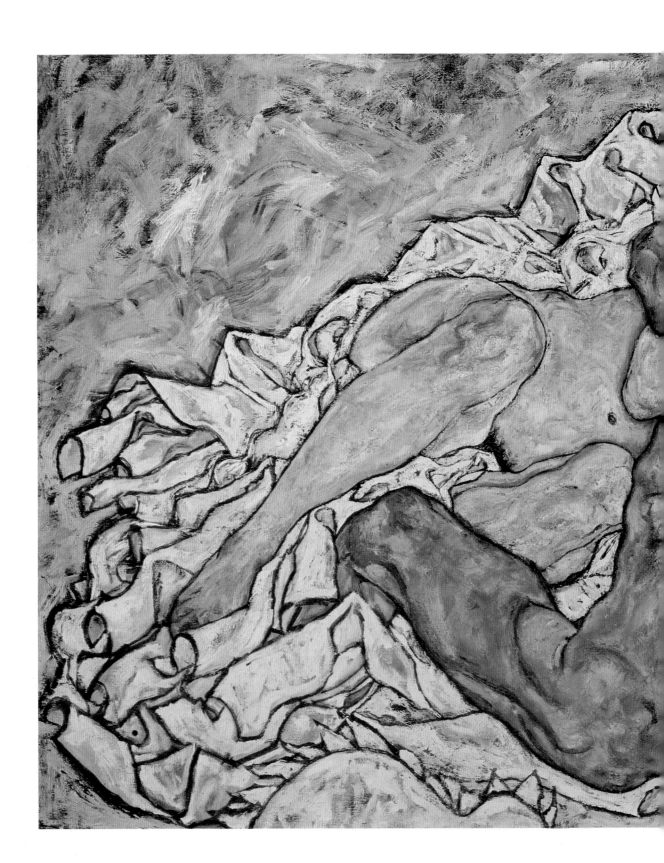